Featuring Illustrations from the
Kids-Did-It! Designs® Kids' Art Collection

The Kids-Did-It! Cook*ie* Book*ie*

(fun)

A Cookie-Baking Cookbook for Kids, Illustrated by Kids!

By Michelle & Glenn Abrams

Published by Kids-Did-It! Properties™

Also by Michelle & Glenn Abrams

Blue Cows & Happy Fruit:
Discovering the Artist in Your Child

Published in the United States by

Kids-Did-It! Properties™
911 Armada Terrace
San Diego, CA 92106 USA

www.kidsdidit.com

Art Direction: Michelle Abrams
Graphic Design: Glenn Abrams

Art Submission Guidelines
and Art Licensing Information:
www.kidsdidit.com

ISBN: 1440455627
EAN-13: 978-1-440-45562-9

Lipstick Face
Jessie Abrams, Age 6

This book is dedicated to my ever enthusiastic spouse and our two remarkable children, Jessie and Nick, without whom this book would never have been conceived.

Glenn & Michelle

Smiling Robot
Nick Abrams, Age 7

Snack Time! Liz Masterson & Megan Albe

Recipes

Blue Squirrel Anna Badger, Age 9

Snack Time!

As a teacher for more than 18 years, Artist and Author, Michelle Abrams, has shared her contagious love for the arts, bringing out the best from her enthusiastic young art students, ages 5 to 14.

Their resulting images are fresh, cute, exuberant, often humorous and quite inspirational - with many worthy of being called 'fine art' in the tradition of *Matisse, Van Gogh, Picasso* or *Miro.*

Of course, in addition to drawing and watercolor lessons, **Snack Time** with its sweet homemade treats was always a studio favorite!

Each of Michelle's Cook*ie* B*ook*ie recipes were inspired and developed to complement the illustrations created by her students so, in addition to a collection of fun, tasty and easy-to-follow baking recipes, this cookbook is also a celebration of the imagination and artistic creativity found in children everywhere!

Butterfly   Jeffrey Shutt, Age 6

Author, Michelle Abrams with daughter, Jessie, testing Cookie Bookie recipes.

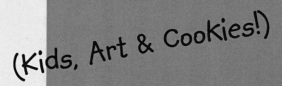

Mix
½ cup
powered
sugar with 2
teaspoons of milk
& drizzle ... the
top of ... cookies.

14

...mmmMMMmmmm... Cookies and Milk!

First Things First

We created the **Cookie Bookie** to be a fun introduction to baking for kids and assume that an adult familiar with simple baking techniques will cook alongside.

For beginners, most of the recipes include icons showing quantity and size relationships, basic measurements and baking times.

We suggest reading through each recipe first, then gathering all the necessary ingredients before you begin. We also recommend that you:

Combine all the **dry** ingredients together before adding them to the **wet** ingredients.

 For best results we also recommend using room temperature eggs, all-purpose flour and room temperature unsalted butter.

Butter

Preheating the oven halfway through preparation can help conserve energy.

Butter from Blue Cows

When rolling cookie dough flat, use a rolling pin on a smooth, dry surface lightly dusted with flour.

To prevent cookies from sticking, spray your baking pan with a non-stick cooking spray or coat it with butter. You can also bake on a piece of cooking parchment paper. Any of these methods will work - and yes, we have tested them all ...many *yummy* times!

Orange Happy Face   Elyse Bobczynski, Age 3

Chipmunks

18 Cookies

Sift Together:
(in a small bowl)

1 ½ Cups Flour +

½ Tsp. Baking Powder

½ Tsp. Baking Soda

½ Tsp. Salt

Beat 'til Fluffy:
(in a LARGE bowl)

½ Cup Butter 1 Stick

½ Cup Granulated Sugar

½ Cup Brown Sugar

Beat In:

1 Egg

1 Tsp. Vanilla Extract

Mix:

Now add flour mixture and mix until blended.

Add:

1 Cup Chocolate Chips

(Optional) ½ Cup Walnuts

Or Macadamia Nuts, or Almonds. No Acorns, please.

Bake 'til Golden:

Drop spoonfuls of dough on a cookie sheet.

15

350°

Bake 14 - 16 minutes

350° Degrees

2

Cherry

18 Cookies

A Bird Elsa Fleisher, Age 8

3

Chirps

Sift Together: (in a small bowl)

- 1 ¾ Cups Flour
- ½ Tsp. Baking Powder
- ½ Tsp. Baking Soda
- ½ Tsp. Salt

Beat 'til Fluffy: (in a LARGE bowl)

- ½ Cup Butter
- ½ Cup Sugar

Beat In:

- 1 Egg
- ½ Tsp. Vanilla Extract

Mix: Now add flour mixture and mix until blended.

Add: 1 Cup Dried Cherries

Form the dough into 1 inch balls, then roll in granulated sugar.

Bake 'til Golden: Place on a cookie sheet. Gently flatten each cookie before topping with ½ Maraschino cherry.

Bake 15 - 17 Minutes

350° Degrees

Peanut Butterflies

10 Butterflies

Sift Together:
(in a small bowl)

1 Cup Flour

½ Tsp. Baking Soda

¼ Tsp. Salt

Beat 'til Fluffy:
(in a LARGE bowl)

¼ Cup Butter 1/2 Stick

¼ Cup Granulated Sugar 1/4 Cup

¼ Cup Brown Sugar 1/4 Cup

1 Egg

½ Tsp. Vanilla

Beat In: 1 Cup Peanut Butter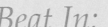
(either chunky or plain)

Mix: Now add flour mixture and mix until blended.

Arrange: Pat hands with flour. Roll 2 big and 2 small dough balls. Press on a cookie sheet, as shown. Add a rolled center body. Dot wings with chocolate chips.

Bake 'til Golden: Bake 12 - 14 Minutes 12

350° Degrees

350°

1.

2.

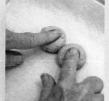

3.

4.

5.

6.

Butterfly Jeffrey Shutt, Age 6

Decorate using your favorite sugar sprinkles and ready-to-use icing!

Red Ladybug Emily Hawk, Age 4

Lady Bug Dots

Sift Together:
(in a small bowl)

1 ¾ Cup Flour 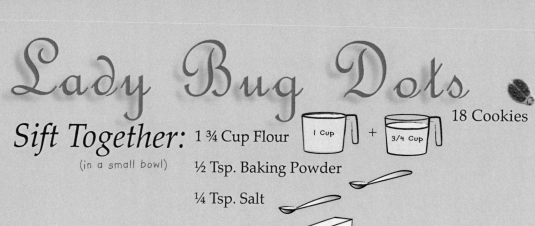 18 Cookies

½ Tsp. Baking Powder

¼ Tsp. Salt

Beat 'til Fluffy:
(in a LARGE bowl)

½ Cup Butter

¾ Cup Granulated Sugar

Beat In:

1 Egg

1 Tsp. Vanilla Extract

Mix:

Now add flour mixture
and mix until blended.

Wrap & Chill:

Scoop sticky dough onto plastic
wrap, cover, and form into a ball.
Refrigerate at least 1 hour.

Roll & Cut:

Roll out the dough ¼" thick
on a lightly floured surface.
Cut out oval-shaped bodies,
then press a small dough ball
on one end to create the head.
Cut a ∧ shape at the other
end.

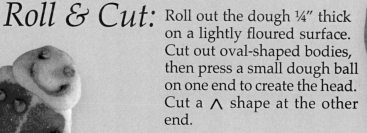

Bake:

Place onto a cookie sheet.

Bake 12 - 14 minutes

350° Degrees

Cool, then decorate.

12

350°

8

Grrr   Andrew Asbille, Age 7

9

DRAGON CRISPS

18 Cookies

Sift Together:
(in a small bowl)

1 ½ Cups Flour

1 Tablespoon Cocoa

1 Tsp. Baking Soda

1 Tsp. Ginger

½ Tsp. Salt

½ Tsp. Cinnamon

Beat 'til Fluffy:
(in a LARGE bowl)

½ Cup Butter

½ Cup Brown Sugar

½ Cup Molasses

Mix: Now add flour mixture and mix until blended.

Shape & Sugar: Roll dough into 2" balls, then gently roll dough balls in sugar.

Place on a Cookie Sheet.

Bake 'til Crispy: Bake 14 - 16 Minutes

350° Degrees

Dino Nick Abrams, Age 12

10

1/2 cup powdered sugar mixed with 2 teaspoons of milk makes a nice shiny glaze. Then decorate with sparkly sugar!

Smiling Star Raquel Bobolia, Age 5

11

Vanilla Stars

12 Cookies

Sift Together:
(in a small bowl)

1 Cup All-Purpose Flour

¼ Tsp. Salt

Beat 'til Fluffy:
(in a LARGE bowl)

½ Cup Butter

¼ Cup Powdered Sugar

1 Tsp. Vanilla

Mix: Now add flour mixture and mix until blended.

Wrap & Chill: Scoop sticky dough onto plastic wrap, cover and form into a ball. Refrigerate for 1 hour.

Roll & Cut: Roll out the dough ¼" thick on a lightly floured surface. Cut the dough into star shapes and place on a cookie sheet.

Bake 'til Golden: Bake 12 - 14 Minutes 350° Degrees

12

350°

Cool, then decorate.

Triangle Tea Treats

24 Cookies

Sift Together: *(in a small bowl)*
- 2 Cups Flour
- ¼ Tsp. Baking Powder
- ¼ Tsp. Salt

Beat 'til Fluffy: *(in a LARGE bowl)*
- ½ Cup Butter — 1 Stick
- ½ Cup Sugar — 1/2 Cup

Beat In:
- 1 Egg
- ½ Tsp. Vanilla
- *(optional)* ½ Tsp. Ground Ginger

Mix: Now add flour mixture and mix until blended.

Add: ¼ Cup Chopped Candied or Crystallized Ginger *(optional)* — 1/4 Cup

Shape & Chill: Scoop dough into plastic wrap, cover and shape into a long triangle log. Refrigerate for 1 hour.

Cut: Cut chilled dough log into ¼" slices and place on a cookie sheet.

Bake 'til Golden: Bake 12 - 14 minutes 350° Degrees

12

350°

13

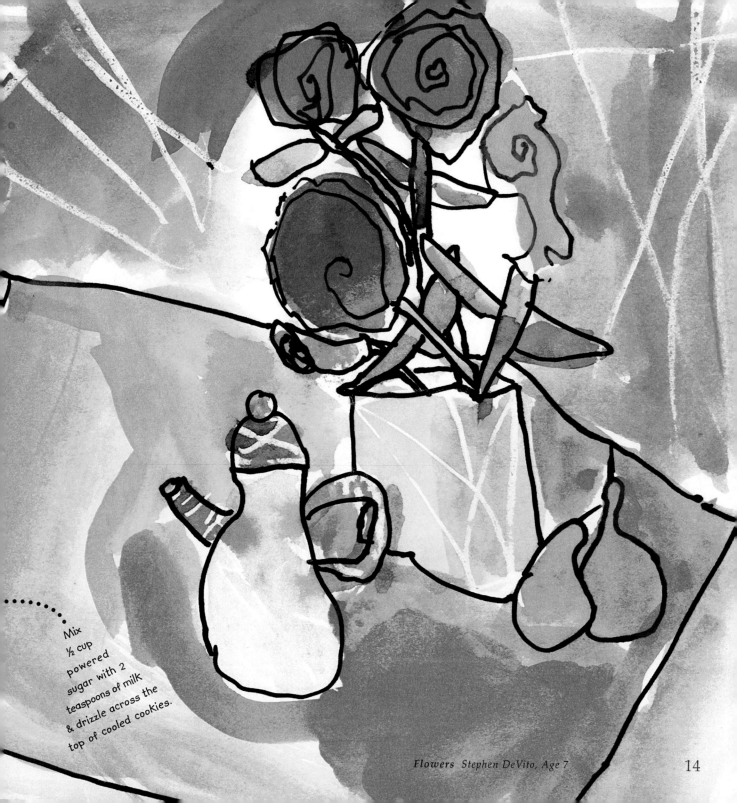

Mix ½ cup powered sugar with 2 teaspoons of milk & drizzle across the top of cooled cookies.

Flowers Stephen DeVito, Age 7

14

15

Pretty Bird Jessie Abrams, Age 12

Bird Nests

18 Nests

Beat 'til Shiny:
(about 2 minutes in a LARGE bowl)

2 Large Egg Whites
(room temperature)

No yolks!

1 Pinch of Salt

¼ Cup Sugar

Gently Fold In:

3 Cups Dry Shredded Coconut, until just mixed together.

Drop spoonfuls onto parchment paper on a cookie sheet.

Bed Time:

With your thumb gently press the center of the cookie to create a bird bed, then sprinkle a few strands of loose coconut on top.

Bake 'til Golden:

Bake 20 - 25 minutes.
325° Degrees

20

325°

Lay Eggs:

Cool! Then add marshmallow chicks or candy eggs.

If you wish, glaze with 1/2 cup powdered sugar mixed with 2 teaspoons of milk and a drop of red food coloring, then top with colored sugar sprinkles.

17   *Heart Maggie McGregor, Age 7*

Sweethearts

Sift Together:
(in a small bowl)

1 ¾ Cups Flour

½ Tsp. Baking Powder

¼ Tsp. Salt

Beat 'til Fluffy:
(in a LARGE bowl)

½ Cup Butter

¾ Cup Granulated Sugar

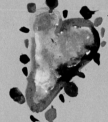

Beat In:

1 Egg

1 Tsp. Vanilla Extract

Mix: Now add flour mixture and mix until blended.

Wrap & Chill: Scoop sticky dough into plastic wrap, cover and form a ball. Chill at least 1 hour.

Roll & Cut: Roll out the dough ¼" thick on a lightly floured surface, then cut into heart shapes and place on a cookie sheet.

Bake 'till Golden: Bake 12 - 14 minutes 350° Degrees

Cool, then decorate.

12

350°

Colorful Heart Bryce Lewis, Age 6

Monster

24 Cookies

Sift Together: 1 Cup Flour
(in a small bowl)

½ Tsp. Salt

½ Tsp. Baking Powder

½ Tsp. Baking Soda

Beat 'til Fluffy: ½ Cup Butter *(1 stick)*
(in a LARGE bowl)

½ Cup Granulated Sugar

½ Cup Brown Sugar

Beat In: 1 Egg

½ Tsp. Vanilla

Mix: Now add flour mixture and mix until blended.

Add Fun Stuff: ½ Cup Oatmeal
(not quick cooking)

1 Cup Chocolate Chips

½ Cup Dried Apricots
(Roughly Chopped)

½ Cup Dried Cranberries
(or Dried Cherries)

1 Cup Toasted Almonds
(Roughly Chopped)

Bake: Spoon onto cookie sheet

Bake 14 - 16 minutes

350° Degrees

Mish-Mashes

Chimera Keaton Raser, Age 8

Choo-Choo-Chewy

Circus Train, Anna Badger, Age 7

Brownies

(Yea! No Beater Required.)

1 Dozen

Melt in Microwave: 1 Cup Chocolate Chips

(75 SECONDS in a LARGE bowl) ¾ Cup Butter

1 Stick   1/2 Stick

Stir: Stir until smooth as chocolate melts.

Add: ¾ Cup Sugar

¾ Cup Brown Sugar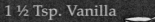

Whisk in: 3 Eggs - one at a time.

1 ½ Tsp. Vanilla

Stir in: ½ Tsp. Salt

¾ Cup Flour

Bake: Butter an 8" x 8" glass baking dish and line with baking parchment.

Coat the parchment with butter or non-stick cooking spray, then pour the batter into the dish.

Bake about 40 minutes

350° Degrees

(until a toothpick poked in the center comes out with just a few crumbs.)

40

350°

Cool & Cut: Let cool completely, then lift out & cut.

(waiting is hard ...but worth it.)

22

Peppermint

Beat 'til Frothy: (in a LARGE bowl)
3 Egg Whites (room temperature) *No yolks!*

Sprinkle:
1 Tsp. Cornstarch

Slowly Beat in:
¾ Cup Granulated Sugar (a tablespoon at a time)
Beat the egg mixture until it's stiff and shiny.

Add in:
½ Tsp. Peppermint Flavor
½ Tsp. White Vinegar
:

Fold In: (using a Spatula)
4 Drops Red Food Coloring

Bake 'til Puffed:
Dollop onto parchment paper on a cookie sheet.
Gently top with Crushed Peppermint.

Preheat the oven. Bake for 1 ½ Hours 200° Degrees

1 ½ Hours — 200°

mmMmm:
Then **turn off** the oven leaving the puffs inside for another hour to set.

1 Hour — 0°

Crispy outside...
Puffy inside...
...mmMmmmm...

Tango Pig Nate Perdue, Age 6   Piggie Sarah Bowen Age 7

Pig Puffs

12 Little Pigs

24

Big Pig Gina Barba, Age 5

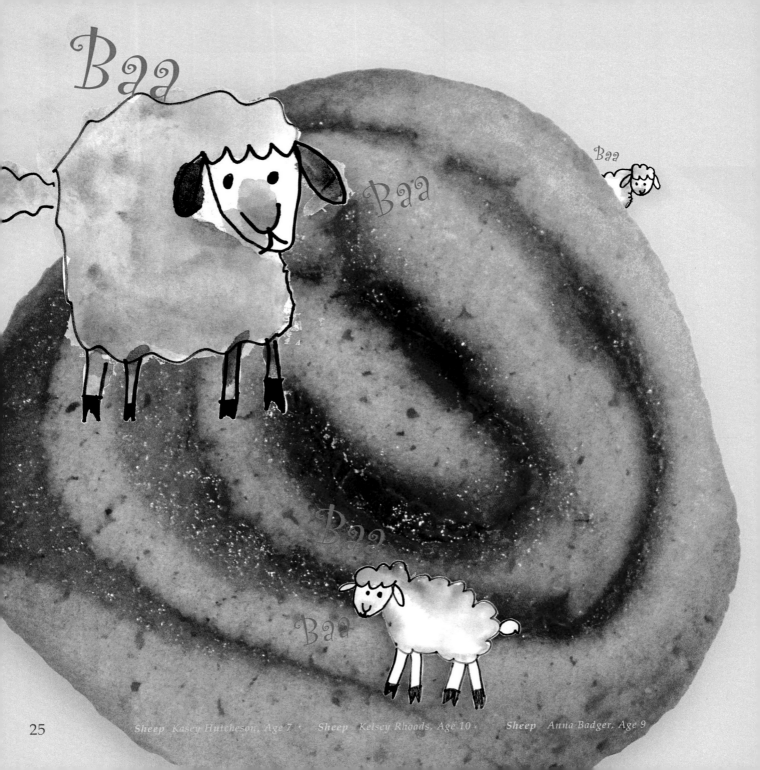

Baa

Baa

Baa

Baa

Baa

Sheep Kasey Hutcheson, Age 7 • *Sheep* Kelsey Rhoads, Age 10 • *Sheep* Anna Badger, Age 9

Lamb Jams

12 Cookies

Sift Together:
(in a small bowl)

1 ¾ Cups Flour

½ Tsp. Baking Powder

¼ Tsp. Salt

Beat 'til Fluffy:
(in a LARGE bowl)

½ Cup Butter

¾ Cup Sugar

Beat In:

1 Egg

1 Tsp. Vanilla Extract

Mix: Now add flour mixture and mix until blended.

Wrap & Chill: Scoop sticky dough onto plastic wrap, cover and form a ball. Chill at least 1 hour.

Roll & Jam: Roll out the dough into a rectangle ¼" thick. Coat with a thin layer of your favorite jam and roll into a log.

Cut: Cut log into ½" thick slices and place on a cookie sheet.

Bake 'til Cute: Bake 14 - 16 minutes 350° Degrees

15

350°

Baa

Baa

Curious Sheep Jeff Shutt, Age 8

Fast Sheep Michele Miller, Age 10

Shy Sheep Stephen DeVito Age 9

Baa

Blue Tailed Sheep
Ashley Mondfrans, Age 11

Sheeped
Emma Griste, Age 7

26

Moon Max Hutcheson, Age 9

Yummmy, our favorite!

Moon Michele Miller, Age 11

27

MOON MELTS

12 Cookies

Sift Together:
(in a small bowl)

1 Cup Flour
1/3 Cup Cocoa
1/4 Tsp. Baking Powder
1/4 Tsp. Salt

Beat 'til Fluffy:
(in a LARGE bowl)

1/2 Cup Butter
1/2 Cup Granulated Sugar

Beat In:

1 Egg
1/2 Tsp. Vanilla Extract

Mix: Now add flour mixture and mix until blended.

Shape & Chill: Scoop the dough into plastic wrap, cover and shape into a 3" diameter log. Refrigerate at least 1 hour.

Cut: Cut log into 1/4" thick slices and place onto a cookie sheet.

Bake: Bake 12 - 14 minutes
350° Degrees

12

350°

Cool 'n Spread: Cool, then dollop Marshmallow Cream between two cookies!

Earth Lauren Van Woy, Age 9

28

29

Art & Artist Index

Sheeped Emma Griste, Age 7

In addition to learning the fundamentals of art and design, every young artist represented in the *Kids-Did-It! Designs*® *kids' art* collection also earns royalties for the reproduction of their work.

For art submission guide-lines, art licensing que-ries and other information, please go to:

www.kidsdidit.com

Art Teacher, Michelle Abrams, assistant Nick & Students

About the Authors

Michelle Abrams
Artist, Art Instructor
Abrams Art Studio

Glenn Abrams
President
Kids-Did-It! Properties

Michelle, a mother of two artists, has a Master of Fine Arts degree from *Yale University* and a broad range of professional experience in the creative arts, including animating for *Sesame Street*, serving as a multimedia Creative Director, and managing her own design studio.

Currently she is a professional painter and art instructor living in Southern California.

www.michelleabrams.com

A graduate of the *Rhode Island School of Design,* throughout his career Glenn has served as Designer, Creative Director and Event Producer on a wide variety of multi-media, marketing communication and entertainment projects.

In 1996 Glenn partnered with his wife, Michelle, to create *Kids-Did-It! Properties*, a California publisher and design studio that also licenses reproduction rights to their growing **Kids-Did-It! Designs®** art collection of fresh and colorful illustrations, most created by Michelle's young art students, ages 3 to 14.

www.kidsdidit.com

Made in the USA
Middletown, DE
20 June 2016